10 MYTHS OF TRADING DEBUNKED

Separating Fact from Fiction

GODFX

Copyright © 2024 GODFX

All rights reserved

The characters and events portrayed in this book are fictitious. Any similarity to real persons, living or dead, is coincidental and not intended by the author.

No part of this book may be reproduced, or stored in a retrieval system, or transmitted in any form or by any means, electronic, mechanical, photocopying, recording, or otherwise, without express written permission of the publisher.

ISBN-13: 9798342439879
ISBN-10: 1477123456

Cover design by: Art Painter
Library of Congress Control Number: 2018675309
Printed in the United States of America

To all the determined traders who dare to break boundaries and chase the dream of financial freedom. May this book guide you through the challenges, ignite your passion, and empower you to build a future of wealth and purpose—not just for yourselves, but for the generations to come.

To the mentors and educators who generously share their wisdom, shaping the future of trading with their insights and support. Your commitment creates a legacy of success, ensuring the growth of the trading community and its lasting influence.

And to my family and friends, whose encouragement and belief have been my greatest strength. Your faith in me has fueled my ambition, and your love has given me the courage to pursue my dreams. This journey is ours together, and I am forever grateful.

"True mastery in trading comes not from predicting the market, but from understanding yourself. The myths you believe are the limits you place on your success."
— GODFX

THIS BOOK IS THE RESULT OF YEARS OF EXPERIENCE, COUNTLESS MISTAKES, AND RELENTLESS DETERMINATION TO UNCOVER THE TRUTHS HIDDEN BENEATH THE MYTHS OF TRADING. ALL INSIGHTS AND LESSONS SHARED HERE ARE DRAWN FROM MY PERSONAL JOURNEY IN THE MARKETS, SHAPED BY BOTH MY FAILURES AND SUCCESSES.

— GODFX

CONTENTS

Title Page

Copyright

Dedication

Epigraph

Foreword

Foreword

Introduction

Preface

Prologue

Untitled

Myth #1 – You'll Get Rich Quick	1
Myth #2 – Trading is Easy Money	7
Myth #3 – You Need a Huge Starting Capital to Trade Successfully	14
Myth #4 – Trading is Gambling & Pure Luck	19
Myth #5 – More Trades Equal More Profits	24
Myth #6 – Successful Traders Win Every Trade	28
Myth #7 – You Need to Predict the Market to Make Money	33
Myth #8 – You Have to Find the Perfect Trade Entry	38
Myth #9 – The More Complicated Your Strategy, the Better Your Results	42

Myth #10 – You Need to Follow Every Bit of Financial News & Constantly Watch the Markets to Succeed	46
11: The Path to Becoming a Better Trader	50
Epilogue	51
Afterword	53
Afterword	55
Acknowledgement	57
About The Author	59
Praise For Author	61
Books In This Series	63
Books By This Author	69
Untitled	75

FOREWORD

Lorem ipsum dolor sit amet, consectetur adipiscing elit, sed do eiusmod tempor incididunt ut labore et dolore magna aliqua. Ut enim ad minim veniam, quis nostrud exercitation ullamco laboris.

FOREWORD

In the vast and often turbulent world of trading, misinformation can be as dangerous as the market's volatility. For years, I have watched traders—both novices and seasoned professionals—fall prey to myths that distort their understanding of what it takes to succeed in this field. It is these misconceptions that can derail even the most dedicated and skilled individuals from achieving their goals.

As a trader, I have experienced firsthand the impact of these myths. I've made mistakes driven by false beliefs, and I've seen others do the same. What I've learned through trial and error is that true mastery of trading requires not only skill and strategy but also a commitment to debunking the myths that hold us back.

That is why I am thrilled to introduce this book. *10 Myths of Trading Debunked* is not just a collection of insights; it is a transformative guide designed to help you navigate the complexities of trading with clarity and purpose. In these pages, you will find a critical examination of the beliefs that often go unchallenged, along with the truths that can set you on a path toward genuine success.

Each chapter delves into a specific myth, revealing the reality behind it and providing actionable strategies to empower you as a trader. You will discover that trading is not about luck or quick riches; it's about discipline, knowledge, and the willingness to learn from both successes and failures.

My journey in trading has been one of continuous learning and growth. I have learned that the most effective traders are those who remain open to questioning their assumptions and adapting their strategies to the ever-changing market landscape. This book encourages you to do just that—challenge the status quo, question the conventional wisdom, and embrace the truths that will ultimately lead to your success.

I want to commend you for taking this step in your trading journey. By reading this book, you are already on the path to becoming a more informed and capable trader. I encourage you to approach these myths with an open mind and to use the insights you gain to refine your trading approach.

Thank you for joining me on this journey of discovery. I am confident that the lessons within these pages will resonate with you, guiding you toward a deeper understanding of trading and helping you to achieve your financial aspirations.

Here's to your success in the markets!

— GODFX

INTRODUCTION

Welcome to *10 Myths of Trading Debunked*. If you're reading this, you're likely on a quest to understand the intricate world of trading, seeking insights that can elevate your performance and lead you toward financial success.

As someone who has navigated the highs and lows of the trading landscape, I can attest that the journey is both thrilling and daunting. It's filled with opportunities and risks, and it demands not just knowledge but a willingness to question conventional wisdom. Throughout my career, I've encountered many traders who have fallen victim to misconceptions that cloud their judgment and hinder their progress. These myths often create false narratives about what it takes to succeed, leading to frustration and discouragement.

In this book, I aim to challenge these myths head-on. Each chapter will explore a specific misconception that has permeated the trading community, providing clarity and insights that can help you build a solid foundation for your trading journey. From the belief that trading is a quick path to wealth to the notion that luck plays a predominant role in success, we'll dissect each myth, uncover the truth, and empower you with practical strategies for navigating the markets.

The truth is, successful trading is not about shortcuts or overnight success. It requires dedication, continuous learning, and a deep understanding of both the markets and yourself. My experiences—filled with both triumphs and setbacks—have taught me invaluable lessons that I wish to share with you.

By debunking these myths, I hope to pave the way for a more informed and resilient approach to trading.

As you delve into this book, I encourage you to keep an open mind. Challenge your beliefs, question what you think you know, and be ready to embrace new perspectives. The road ahead may be challenging, but with the right mindset and knowledge, you can overcome obstacles and achieve your trading goals.

Thank you for allowing me to be a part of your journey. Let's begin the process of uncovering the truths that will guide you toward becoming a more effective and successful trader.

— GODFX

PREFACE

In the world of trading, myths and misconceptions abound, often leading aspiring traders astray. As I look back on my journey, I realize that many of the challenges I faced were rooted in these very myths. I wrote this book to illuminate the truths that lie beneath the surface and to help you navigate the complexities of the trading landscape with confidence.

From the moment I stepped into the financial markets, I was captivated by the potential for success and the allure of financial freedom. However, I quickly learned that trading is not just about making money; it's a discipline that requires a deep understanding of both the markets and oneself. Along the way, I encountered numerous myths that almost derailed my progress. These false beliefs often led to impulsive decisions and costly mistakes.

With *10 Myths of Trading Debunked,* my goal is to challenge these misconceptions and provide you with a clearer perspective on what it truly means to be a successful trader. Each chapter is dedicated to dismantling a common myth, revealing the reality that often lies hidden behind it. Through my experiences, I hope to empower you to recognize these myths in your own trading journey and to develop a more informed and effective approach.

Trading is not merely a set of rules or strategies; it is an evolving art that demands patience, discipline, and continuous learning. The market is a living entity, and understanding its nuances requires dedication and resilience. As you explore the myths presented in this book, I encourage you to reflect on your own beliefs and assumptions. Challenge what you think you know, and be open to new ideas that may enhance your trading journey.

Remember, the path to becoming a successful trader is not a straight line. It is filled with ups and downs, triumphs and setbacks. By debunking these myths, I hope to equip you with the tools and insights needed to navigate the inevitable challenges ahead.

Thank you for joining me on this journey. Together, let's uncover the truths that will pave the way for your success in the world of trading.

— GODFX

PROLOGUE

In the realm of trading, where fortunes can shift in an instant, the line between success and failure is often drawn by perception. As I embarked on my trading journey, I quickly discovered that the most formidable barriers were not the markets themselves, but the myths and misconceptions that clouded my understanding.

These myths often masquerade as truths, luring even the most determined traders into a web of self-doubt and poor decision-making. I've seen brilliant minds falter because they believed they needed to "outsmart" the market, that trading was a gamble rather than a calculated endeavor. I've witnessed others cling to the illusion of instant wealth, only to watch their dreams slip away when faced with reality.

As I navigated my path, I realized that breaking free from these myths was crucial to my development as a trader. I learned that the journey is not about mastering complex strategies or perfecting technical analysis; it's about cultivating the right mindset and understanding the true nature of trading. It's about recognizing that success comes from discipline, patience, and an unwavering commitment to continuous learning.

This book is born from my desire to share the hard-earned wisdom I've gained through experience. I want to help you see beyond the illusions and equip you with the knowledge to make informed decisions in your trading endeavors. Each chapter is dedicated to debunking a specific myth, providing you with insights and practical strategies to navigate the trading landscape more effectively.

As you read through these pages, I encourage you to reflect on your own beliefs and assumptions. Ask yourself: Are you holding on to any myths that may be hindering your progress? This book is not just about dispelling misconceptions; it's about empowering you to take control of your trading journey and to build a foundation for lasting success.

Thank you for embarking on this journey with me. Let's uncover the truths that will not only reshape your understanding of trading but also propel you toward achieving your financial aspirations.

— GODFX

UNTITLED

MYTH #1 – YOU'LL GET RICH QUICK

The biggest myth I see time and time again is the idea that trading is a fast track to wealth. This myth is dangerous because it encourages traders to take unnecessary risks in the hopes of hitting it big overnight. But the reality is quite different.

Trading requires time, patience, and discipline. Successful traders understand that it's not about making a fortune in a single trade, but about building wealth slowly and steadily over time. Think of trading like growing a tree—each trade is a seed you plant, and over time, with the right care and attention, it will grow. But it won't happen overnight.

Actionable Steps to Overcome the 'Get Rich Quick' Mentality

It's not enough to simply recognize the "get rich quick" myth in trading. You need a clear, structured approach to replace it with a more sustainable mindset and practice. Let's break down each actionable step in more detail, so you have practical, actionable strategies to guide you toward long-term success.

1. Set Long-Term Goals

A critical part of shifting away from the "get rich quick" mentality is focusing on long-term goals. Without a clear roadmap, it's easy to get distracted by short-term gains, which leads to impulsive decisions.

How to Set Long-Term Goals:

Define What Success Looks Like:
Ask yourself, "What do I want to achieve in the next year, five years, or even ten years?" Success doesn't necessarily mean doubling your money overnight. It could mean hitting a certain percentage of growth in your portfolio annually, mastering a specific trading strategy, or gradually increasing your trade size.

Set Realistic Financial Targets:
It's important to establish measurable and realistic financial goals. For example, instead of saying, "I want to make a million dollars," you can aim for a 10-15% return on investment per year. This may not sound as exciting, but compounded over time, such returns can be incredibly powerful.

Break Down Larger Goals:
Once you've set a larger goal, break it down into smaller, more achievable milestones. This makes the path forward clearer and keeps you focused on steady progress. For example, if your goal is to achieve a 15% annual return, divide that into quarterly or monthly goals, like 3% per quarter.

Track and Adjust:
Review your progress regularly. Evaluate what's working and what's not. Are your goals still realistic? If you've been too conservative or overly ambitious, adjust your targets and strategies accordingly. Consistency is key, so be flexible when necessary.

2. Develop a Trading Plan
A detailed trading plan is essential to long-term success and helps eliminate emotional decision-making. This plan will serve as your

guide to every trade you make, ensuring that your actions align with your goals.

What Should Be in Your Trading Plan?

Risk Management:
Protecting your capital should be your top priority. Determine how much of your account you are willing to risk on each trade. The common rule is to risk only 1-2% of your total trading account on any single trade. This ensures that no single loss can wipe out your account.

Define Entry and Exit Rules:
A trading plan should include clear criteria for entering and exiting trades. This could be based on technical analysis (e.g., moving averages, RSI levels) or fundamental analysis (e.g., earnings reports, economic data). When will you enter a trade, and more importantly, when will you exit? Stick to these rules no matter what emotions say.

Trade Size:
Determine the position size for each trade based on your risk tolerance. Larger positions can lead to larger profits but also larger losses, so balance is key. Use a position-sizing calculator to ensure that you're not overexposed in any one trade.

Stop-Loss and Take-Profit Levels:
Predefine your stop-loss (how much you're willing to lose) and take-profit (how much profit you're aiming to make) levels before entering any trade. This will help you stay disciplined and prevent emotions from dictating your decisions during a trade.

Review and Reflect:
Continuously review your trading performance. Keep a trading journal to document the reasons behind each trade, its outcome, and what you learned. By consistently analysing your trades, you

can identify strengths and weaknesses in your approach.

Benefits of a Trading Plan:

Reduces Emotional Trading:
By following your predefined rules, you reduce the likelihood of making impulsive decisions based on emotions like greed or fear.

Increases Consistency:
A solid plan allows you to be consistent in your approach, which is essential for long-term success. It removes guesswork from the process.

Improves Discipline:
Sticking to a plan forces discipline. Even when markets are volatile, and emotions run high, a good trader sticks to their plan.

3. Embrace Compounding Growth

Understanding the power of compounding growth can transform how you view trading. Compounding is the process by which profits generated from your trades are reinvested to generate even more profits. The key is to focus on small, consistent gains that will multiply over time.

How Compounding Works:

Start with Modest Gains:
Let's say you have a $10,000 trading account and you aim for a 1% profit per week. That's only $100 a week, which might not sound like much. But over the course of a year, with compounding, your account would grow substantially—far beyond just adding $100 per week.

Reinvest Profits:
The secret to compounding lies in reinvesting your profits. Each time you make a profit, add it back into your trading capital, so

that your future trades are larger and can generate even bigger returns.

Long-Term Focus:
Compounding works best when you focus on long-term growth rather than short-term gains. By consistently reinvesting and allowing time to magnify your gains, the returns will be significantly larger in the long run.

Example of Compounding Growth:
Let's break down how compounding works in a simple example:
- Initial Capital: $10,000
- Weekly Return Goal: 1%
- Weeks in a Year: 52
- Final Capital at Year End (with compounding): $17,450

A modest 1% per week doesn't sound like much, but by reinvesting profits consistently, you can achieve a 74.5% gain over the course of the year, resulting in significant growth.

Benefits of Compounding:

Exponential Growth:
Small, consistent gains can add up to substantial results over time, far outpacing irregular, large wins followed by large losses.

Promotes Patience:
Focusing on compounding encourages a patient, long-term perspective, which helps you avoid the temptation of risky, short-term trades.

Reduces Stress:
When you understand that small wins can lead to big outcomes, you're less likely to feel pressured into making risky moves. You can stay calm, knowing that your strategy will pay off over time.

Final Thoughts

Overcoming the "get rich quick" myth requires a disciplined, methodical approach. By setting long-term goals, developing a solid trading plan, and embracing the power of compounding growth, you can shift your focus from chasing short-term gains to building lasting wealth. Trading isn't about hitting the jackpot with one lucky trade. It's about playing the long game, planting seeds, and nurturing your investments over time.

These actionable steps not only protect you from emotional trading but also guide you toward sustainable success in the markets. Focus on steady, manageable growth, and your portfolio will flourish over the long term.

MYTH #2 – TRADING IS EASY MONEY

It's not uncommon to see social media influencers and traders flashing their profits online, making it seem like trading is the easiest way to make money. Don't be fooled. Trading is hard work. It requires an understanding of technical and fundamental analysis, market psychology, and risk management. If it were easy, everyone would be a millionaire. The truth is, trading is a skill that takes years to master. And like any skill, it requires dedication, learning from mistakes, and adapting to the ever-changing markets.

Actionable Steps to Overcome the 'Easy Money' Mentality
To succeed in trading, you need to approach it like a professional and treat it with the seriousness it deserves. Let's break down each actionable step that will help you develop the necessary skills and discipline to become a successful trader.

1. Invest in Your Education
Education is the foundation for success in any field, and trading is no exception. The more you know, the better equipped you are to make informed decisions in the market. Many novice traders jump into trading without a solid understanding of how markets work, relying on luck or following online trends. This often leads

to failure.

How to Invest in Your Trading Education:

Study Technical Analysis:
Technical analysis involves studying price charts, indicators, and patterns to forecast future price movements. This is essential for understanding market behaviour and timing trades. Start by learning about common indicators like moving averages, RSI (Relative Strength Index), MACD (Moving Average Convergence Divergence), and support/resistance levels. You should also familiarize yourself with candlestick patterns, trend analysis, and volume indicators.

Study Fundamental Analysis:
Fundamental analysis involves evaluating the financial health and overall value of a company (for stocks) or macroeconomic data (for forex and commodities). This helps you understand the bigger picture and long-term market trends. Learn how to read balance sheets, income statements, and economic reports like GDP, unemployment rates, and interest rates. For stock traders, researching earnings reports and understanding the business model is key.

Enrol in Courses and Webinars:
Consider enrolling in online courses or attending webinars led by professional traders. Platforms like Udemy, Coursera, and Investopedia offer comprehensive courses in both technical and fundamental analysis. Some brokerages and trading platforms also offer free educational resources, tutorials, and community forums to enhance your learning.

Read Books and Follow Experts:
There are countless books that cover different aspects of trading. Some must-read books include *"Technical Analysis of the Financial Markets"* by John Murphy, *"Trading for a Living"* by Alexander Elder,

and *"Market Wizards"* by Jack Schwager. Following experienced traders on platforms like Twitter, LinkedIn, and financial news outlets can also provide valuable insights into current market conditions and strategies.

Practice with Demo Accounts:
Most trading platforms offer demo accounts where you can practice trading with virtual money. Use these accounts to test your strategies and develop your skills without the risk of losing real capital. Treat your demo account like its real money—this will help you learn risk management and improve your trading discipline.

Benefits of Education:

Increased Confidence:
 A deep understanding of the markets boosts your confidence in your decision-making process. You'll be more prepared to navigate market fluctuations.

Informed Decision-Making:
 Instead of relying on luck or market hype, you'll base your trades on analysis and data, leading to more informed and rational trading decisions.

Long-Term Success:
Trading is a long game, and continuous education allows you to evolve with the markets. The more you know, the better equipped you'll be to adapt to new trends and strategies.

2. Track Your Trades
Successful traders don't just rely on memory to improve—they meticulously track and review their trades. Maintaining a trading journal is one of the most powerful tools for self-improvement. It helps you identify patterns, learn from your mistakes, and build on your successes.

How to Track Your Trades:

Maintain a Detailed Trading Journal:
Every time you make a trade, document the details of that trade. Include:

Date and Time: When you entered and exited the trade.

Asset Traded: The stock, forex pair, commodity, or other asset.

Entry and Exit Prices: The price at which you bought and sold.

Position Size: How much capital you committed to the trade.

Reason for Trade: Why you entered the trade—technical indicators, market news, or other factors.

Profit/Loss: The outcome of the trade and percentage return on investment (ROI).

Emotional State: How did you feel during the trade—confident, anxious, excited, fearful? This helps you understand how emotions affect your decisions.

Review Your Journal Regularly:
It's not enough to just record your trades; you need to review them. Weekly or monthly reviews will help you identify patterns in your trading behaviour. Are you consistently making impulsive trades based on emotions? Are certain times of the day or specific assets more profitable for you? Regular reviews will help you pinpoint areas for improvement.

Analyse Your Mistakes:
Mistakes are inevitable in trading, but the key to success is learning from them. When you make a loss, analyse why it

happened. Did you ignore your stop-loss? Were you following a market trend without proper analysis? Did emotions cloud your judgment? Identifying mistakes will help you avoid repeating them in the future.

Celebrate Wins and Refine Your Strategy:
When you have a winning trade, don't just move on. Analyse why that trade was successful. Was it because of thorough research? Did you stick to your trading plan? Celebrate your wins and refine your strategy to replicate your success.

Benefits of Tracking Your Trades:

Improved Discipline:
A trading journal forces you to be more disciplined by holding yourself accountable for every trade.

Enhanced Self-Awareness:
Tracking your trades helps you understand your strengths and weaknesses, as well as how emotions impact your decision-making.

Constant Learning:
By regularly reviewing your trades, you engage in continuous learning and improvement, leading to better results over time.

3. Manage Risk
Risk management is the backbone of successful trading. Without it, even the most skilled traders can lose everything in a short amount of time. The key to longevity in trading is protecting your capital and minimizing losses.

How to Manage Risk in Trading:

Use the 1% or 2% Rule:
Never risk more than 1-2% of your total trading account on any

single trade. This ensures that even if you lose a trade, it won't have a significant impact on your overall portfolio. For example, if you have a $10,000 account, you should only risk $100-$200 on any given trade.

Set Stop-Loss Orders:
A stop-loss is a predetermined price level at which you'll exit a trade to limit your losses. Always set a stop-loss before entering any trade, and never move it further away to avoid closing a losing position. Stick to your predetermined risk tolerance.

Calculate Risk-Reward Ratios:
Before entering any trade, calculate the risk-reward ratio, which compares how much you're risking versus how much you stand to gain. A typical risk-reward ratio might be 1:2, meaning you're risking $100 to potentially gain $200. Only take trades where the potential reward outweighs the risk.

Diversify Your Trades:
Don't put all your money into one trade or asset. Diversifying across different assets or sectors reduces your exposure to risk. For example, don't have all your capital in tech stocks or just forex. Spread your investments to mitigate the impact of a loss in one area.

Avoid Over-Leveraging:
Leverage allows you to control larger positions with a small amount of capital, but it also increases your potential losses. Many beginner traders over-leverage, leading to massive losses. Use leverage cautiously and understand the risks before using it.

Benefits of Managing Risk:

Preserves Capital:
  Proper risk management ensures that you can withstand multiple losing trades without wiping out your entire account.

Increases Longevity:
Risk management allows you to stay in the game long enough to learn, improve, and eventually become consistently profitable.

Reduces Stress:
Knowing that you have predefined limits on how much you can lose on any given trade can reduce emotional stress and prevent you from panicking when the market moves against you.

Conclusion
Trading is far from easy money. It requires education, experience, and most importantly, discipline. By investing in your education, tracking your trades, and managing your risk, you will not only avoid falling into the "easy money" trap but also position yourself for long-term success. The road to becoming a successful trader is challenging, but with these actionable steps, you'll be better equipped to navigate the complexities of the markets.

MYTH #3 – YOU NEED A HUGE STARTING CAPITAL TO TRADE SUCCESSFULLY

This is one of the myths that stops most people from even attempting to trade. The belief that you need a massive amount of capital to get started is simply untrue.
In today's world, you can start with as little as a few hundred dollars. The key isn't the size of your starting capital, but how well you manage it. With proper risk management and the right strategies, you can grow a small account into something significant.

Actionable Steps for Growing a Small Trading Account
The following steps will guide you in managing a small trading account effectively and maximizing its growth potential, without the misconception that more capital equals automatic success.

1. Start Small, Scale Gradually
Starting small allows you to learn the ropes without risking too much of your capital. Many traders lose big by taking on large positions too early, before fully understanding the risks involved.

Starting with a smaller amount forces you to be more precise with your trades, which in turn teaches discipline.

How to Scale Gradually:

Begin with a Small Investment:
It's wise to start with just a few hundred dollars. This helps you get a feel for how the markets work without the pressure of losing a significant portion of your savings. Many brokers offer accounts with no minimum deposit, so you can ease into the process with small trades.

Test Your Strategy with Small Trades:
Starting small also allows you to test your trading strategies without the risk of large losses. Focus on making consistently profitable trades, even if the gains are minimal. This builds a foundation of confidence and discipline, which will be crucial when you increase your position sizes.

Reinvest Profits to Scale:
As you build a track record of success, gradually increase the size of your trades. Reinvesting a portion of your profits is a safe and effective way to scale. For example, if you grow your account by 10%, consider increasing your trade sizes by 10% as well. This ensures that your growth is proportional to your account's performance.

Avoid Over-Leveraging:
Leverage allows you to control a larger position with a small amount of capital, but it also increases your risk. Avoid the temptation to over-leverage when starting small, as this can lead to larger losses than you can handle. Instead, use conservative leverage to maintain control over your trades.

2. Use Proper Position Sizing
Position sizing refers to determining the number of shares,

contracts, or lots to trade based on the size of your account and your risk tolerance. The goal is to ensure that no single trade can wipe out your account, especially when you're starting with a small amount of capital.

How to Implement Proper Position Sizing:

Follow the 1% or 2% Rule:
One of the golden rules of trading is to never risk more than 1-2% of your account on any single trade. This means that if you have a $1,000 trading account, you should only risk $10 to $20 per trade. This prevents a string of losses from drastically reducing your capital.

Calculate Trade Size Based on Risk:
To determine how large a position to take, calculate the distance between your entry price and stop-loss. For example, if your stop-loss is $0.50 below your entry price, and you are willing to risk $20 on the trade, you would buy 40 shares ($20 ÷ $0.50 = 40 shares). This approach ensures that your risk is controlled and consistent.

Adjust for Market Conditions:
If the market is volatile, reduce the size of your positions. Volatile markets can lead to larger price swings, increasing the chance of hitting your stop-loss. By reducing your position size, you reduce the potential for large losses.

Stick to Your Strategy:
As tempting as it might be to increase your trade size after a winning streak, discipline is key. Continue using proper position sizing to protect your account from unexpected market movements or reversals.

3. Focus on Capital Preservation
When trading with a small account, your first priority should

always be to protect your capital. Without capital, you can't trade, and protecting it ensures you can survive the inevitable losses that come with trading. The goal isn't just to grow your account, but to keep it intact during drawdowns.

How to Preserve Your Capital:

Set Strict Stop-Loss Orders:
Stop-loss orders automatically close your position when the price reaches a certain level, limiting your losses. Always use a stop-loss to protect your capital, especially when trading with a smaller account. This ensures that no trade can inflict too much damage on your overall account balance.

Avoid Over-Trading:
It's common for beginners to over-trade, thinking that more trades equal more profit. However, over-trading increases your exposure to risk and can quickly deplete your capital due to transaction fees and losses. Be selective with your trades and focus on quality setups rather than quantity.

Trade with a Risk-Reward Ratio in Mind:
Always look for trades where the potential reward is greater than the risk. A typical rule is to aim for a 2:1 or 3:1 risk-reward ratio. For example, if you are risking $20, look for trades where you can potentially make $40 to $60. This ensures that even if you lose more trades than you win, your profitable trades will make up for the losses.

Stay Calm During Drawdowns:
Every trader experiences drawdowns, where the account balance decreases due to a series of losses. During these periods, it's crucial not to panic or try to "win back" losses by increasing your risk. Stick to your risk management strategy and trust that your disciplined approach will help you recover over time.

Final Thoughts

Starting with a small trading account doesn't mean you can't achieve significant success. With the right strategies, proper risk management, and a focus on capital preservation, you can grow even a modest account into something substantial over time. The key is to start small, learn as you go, and scale your trades gradually. By using proper position sizing and focusing on protecting your capital, you'll ensure that you stay in the game long enough to see meaningful growth. Remember, it's not about how much you start with, but how well you manage and grow what you have.

MYTH #4 – TRADING IS GAMBLING & PURE LUCK

It's easy to label trading as gambling, especially for those who don't understand it. But unlike gambling, where outcomes are purely based on chance, trading involves skill, knowledge, and calculated risk.

The best traders rely on their strategies, understanding of market conditions, and solid risk management practices. I've seen people lose money because they treated trading like a casino, betting their capital on "hunches" or unproven strategies. Successful trading requires preparation, discipline, and a clear approach to risk management.

Actionable Steps to Shift from Gambling to Trading with Strategy

To break away from the misconception that trading is pure luck, here's how you can incorporate structure and strategy into your trading approach:

1. Develop a Trading Strategy

A solid trading strategy is the foundation of any successful trading career. Rather than relying on guesswork or market rumors, base your trades on a well-researched plan that's tailored to your goals, risk tolerance, and trading style.

How to Build and Stick to a Strategy:

Technical Analysis:
Learn to read price charts and use technical indicators such as moving averages, RSI, MACD, and Fibonacci retracements. These tools can help you identify trends, entry, and exit points, as well as areas of potential price reversal. Technical analysis is vital for short-term trading as it helps predict future price movements based on historical data.

Fundamental Analysis:
If you prefer longer-term trades or investing, fundamental analysis is crucial. This involves evaluating a company's financial health, industry conditions, earnings reports, and macroeconomic factors to assess its intrinsic value. This analysis can help you identify whether an asset is overvalued or undervalued, providing you with strategic entry points for trades.

Back test Your Strategy:
Before implementing any strategy with real capital, back test it using historical data. This allows you to see how it would have performed in various market conditions and tweak it if necessary. Many online platforms offer tools that let you back test your strategy in a simulated environment.

Stick to Your Strategy:
One of the biggest mistakes traders make is abandoning their strategy after a few losing trades. Consistency is key. If your strategy is sound and backed by analysis, stick with it. Discipline will prevent you from making impulsive, emotion-driven decisions.

2. Focus on Probabilities

Trading isn't about being right all the time—it's about managing risk and placing trades where the odds are in your favor. While there's no way to predict market movements with absolute certainty, understanding probabilities allows you to make more informed decisions and manage risk effectively.

How to Manage Risk and Play the Probabilities:

Risk-Reward Ratio:
Always consider the risk-reward ratio before entering a trade. This ratio compares the potential reward of a trade with the risk involved. For instance, a 2:1 risk-reward ratio means you're risking $1 to potentially gain $2. By maintaining favourable risk-reward ratios, you can ensure that even if you lose more trades than you win, the profitable trades will cover your losses and then some.

Win Rate and Expectancy:
Your win rate is the percentage of your trades that are profitable. Your expectancy is the average amount you can expect to win or lose per trade. Even if your win rate is below 50%, having a high expectancy (through strong risk-reward ratios) can still lead to profitability over time.

Position Sizing:
Use position sizing to manage the amount of risk you take on each trade. Never put all your capital into a single trade. Instead, limit the amount of your capital allocated to each trade, typically risking only 1-2% of your total capital. This ensures that no single trade will wipe out your account.

3. Don't Rely on Luck—Stay Disciplined and Follow Your Rules
While the market can sometimes behave unpredictably, a disciplined approach based on well-thought-out rules will always outperform one based on whims or luck. Emotional or impulsive trading usually leads to losses, as decisions driven by fear or greed

often cloud judgment.

How to Maintain Discipline and Follow Trading Rules:
Create Clear Trading Rules:
Define clear entry and exit criteria, based on your strategy. For example, you might decide only to enter a trade when a specific technical indicator gives a buy signal, or exit when your price target is hit. Having predefined rules removes emotion from the equation and keeps you consistent.

Use Stop-Loss Orders:
Always have a plan to limit your losses on each trade by setting stop-loss orders. These automatically exit your position once a certain loss threshold is reached, protecting you from large, unexpected market movements. Never remove or widen your stop-loss out of hope that the market will turn in your favour.

Avoid Revenge Trading:
One of the biggest emotional pitfalls traders fall into is revenge trading—making impulsive trades to recover from a loss. This leads to irrational decisions and even greater losses. After a losing trade, take a step back, review what went wrong, and stick to your plan before entering another trade.

Journal Your Trades:
Keeping a detailed trading journal allows you to analyse your successes and failures over time. Record why you entered a trade, how you felt, and whether or not you followed your plan. This reflection will help you improve your discipline and trading decisions over the long term.

Final Thoughts
Trading can seem like gambling to those who approach it without structure or discipline. However, with the right mindset, proper strategies, and risk management techniques, trading becomes a calculated activity rather than a game of luck. By

focusing on strategy development, understanding probabilities, and maintaining discipline, you can set yourself apart from traders who rely on luck and emotional decisions. The key is to stay patient, keep learning, and approach every trade with a methodical and professional attitude.

MYTH #5 – MORE TRADES EQUAL MORE PROFITS

More trades don't mean more profits. In fact, overtrading can lead to massive losses. Many traders fall into the trap of thinking that staying active in the market will result in more gains, but that's not true.

What matters is quality, not quantity. A well-timed, well-executed trade will outperform dozens of hasty or ill-advised trades. I've experienced this firsthand—some of my most profitable periods came from trading less, not more.

Actionable Steps to Combat Overtrading

Here's how you can avoid the trap of overtrading and focus on maximizing the quality of each trade rather than quantity:

1. Be Selective: Only Take Trades That Align with Your Strategy

Patience and selectivity are essential in successful trading. Rather than chasing every potential trade, focus on high-probability setups that align with your trading plan. Each trade should have a clear rationale and meet specific criteria before execution.

How to Be More Selective in Your Trading:

Follow Your Trading Plan:
Only enter trades that meet the criteria outlined in your strategy. For example, you might only trade when certain technical indicators align or when specific market conditions are present. If a trade doesn't align with your pre-defined rules, skip it, no matter how tempting it may seem.

Avoid Emotional Trades:
Many traders fall into the habit of trading based on fear of missing out (FOMO) or revenge trading after a loss. These impulsive decisions often result in poorly timed entries and exits. Stick to your plan and avoid trades that don't have a solid analytical basis.

Trade Fewer Markets:
Focusing on too many markets or assets can spread your attention too thin. Stick to a few key markets or instruments that you understand well. This will allow you to focus on finding the best opportunities rather than trading just for the sake of being active.

Use Filters:
Implement filters to screen out poor setups. For instance, you can choose to trade only when the market volatility reaches a certain level or when price moves in a particular direction. This way, you minimize the number of potential trades and focus on only the best ones.

2. Avoid Overtrading: Focus on High-Probability Setups

Overtrading occurs when you enter the market too often, often without enough reason or proper analysis. Instead of focusing on frequent trades, place your attention on those that offer the highest probability of success based on your trading strategy. Fewer, high-quality trades will almost always outperform frequent, lower-quality ones.

How to Focus on High-Probability Setups:

Set Strict Entry Criteria:
Define your entry criteria clearly and follow them without exception. These could include specific chart patterns, price action signals, or certain technical indicators. By using strict rules, you ensure that each trade has a higher probability of success rather than jumping in without sufficient reasoning.

Track Your Success Rate:
Use your trading journal to analyse past trades and identify which setups have been the most successful. By focusing on these high-probability setups, you can reduce the number of trades you take and focus only on those with the best chance of success.

Use Alerts:
Set up alerts for when specific market conditions meet your criteria. This allows you to stay out of the market during periods of inactivity or low-quality setups and only act when your conditions are met. It prevents the temptation to enter trades just to be active.

3. Practice Patience: Wait for the Best Opportunities

Patience is one of the most underrated traits in trading. The desire to always be active can lead to taking subpar trades that don't align with your strategy. However, waiting for the best setups allows you to trade with more precision and confidence, ultimately leading to better results.

How to Be More Patient and Wait for Quality Trades:
Understand Market Conditions:
Not every market condition is favourable for trading. Sometimes it's best to sit on the sidelines when the market is choppy or unclear. Recognize when the market conditions are conducive to your strategy, and be comfortable sitting out when they aren't.

Think Long-Term:

Adopt a long-term mindset rather than focusing on short-term gains. This will help you avoid the constant need for action and allow you to wait for the best opportunities. Successful trading isn't about making money every day, but about making smart trades over time.

Reduce Screen Time:
Overwatching the markets can lead to impulsive decisions and the temptation to enter trades prematurely. Reduce screen time by stepping away from the charts periodically. Use alerts or automated trading systems to help manage your trades without constantly watching the market.

Visualize Missed Trades as Learning Opportunities:
Sometimes the best lesson comes from trades you didn't take. Reflect on why you chose to sit out, whether the trade ended up being successful or not, and how it aligns with your strategy. This reflection process will enhance your ability to be patient in the future.

Final Thoughts
More trades don't necessarily lead to more profits. In fact, successful trading is often about waiting for the right opportunities, not rushing into the market. By being more selective, avoiding overtrading, and practicing patience, you'll be able to improve your performance and avoid the pitfalls of quantity-driven trading. Focus on the quality of your trades, and you'll find that fewer, well-executed trades can bring more consistent and significant profits over time.

MYTH #6 – SUCCESSFUL TRADERS WIN EVERY TRADE

No trader wins every trade—not even the best in the world. Losses are part of the game, and the sooner you accept that, the sooner you can become a more successful trader. What separates successful traders from the rest is not the number of winning trades, but how they manage their losses.
When I lose on a trade, I don't panic. I understand that it's part of the process, and I focus on making sure my losses are smaller than my wins. The key is consistency, risk management, and learning from each mistake.

Actionable Steps for Managing Losses and Achieving Long-Term Profitability
To become a successful trader, it's crucial to focus on managing losses rather than avoiding them entirely. Here's how you can implement effective strategies to stay profitable even when you encounter losing trades:

1. Accept Losses: Don't Let Losses Affect Your Trading Psychology
One of the most important traits of a successful trader is

the ability to accept losses without letting them influence future decisions negatively. Losses are inevitable in trading, and becoming emotionally attached to them can lead to poor decision-making.

How to Accept Losses and Maintain a Balanced Mindset:

Reframe Losses as Learning Experiences:
Each loss is an opportunity to learn. Analyze your losing trades without emotion—did you follow your trading plan, or did you deviate? By reflecting on your mistakes, you can adjust and improve your strategy moving forward.

Avoid Revenge Trading:
Revenge trading occurs when you try to "get back" the money you lost by immediately entering another trade without a sound reason. This is a dangerous emotional reaction that often results in more losses. After a losing trade, take a break, reassess the market, and stick to your strategy before making any further decisions.

Stick to the Plan:
Losses can sometimes make traders question their strategy or lead to impulsive decisions to change it. While it's important to adjust your strategy based on results, don't make knee-jerk changes based on one or two losses. Stick to your long-term plan and maintain consistency, which is key to overcoming short-term setbacks.

Use Positive Self-Talk:
Trading can be mentally exhausting, especially after a loss. Stay positive by reminding yourself that losses are a natural part of trading. Over time, these setbacks will become easier to handle if you keep a positive attitude and focus on the bigger picture.

2. Limit Losses: Use Stop-Loss Orders to Minimize the Impact of

Losing Trades

Managing risk is the cornerstone of successful trading. While you cannot control the market, you can control how much of your capital you are willing to lose on any given trade. One of the most effective ways to limit losses is through the use of stop-loss orders, which automatically exit a trade when the price hits a predetermined level.

How to Set and Use Stop-Loss Orders Effectively:

Predefine Your Risk for Each Trade:
Before entering a trade, always decide how much you are willing to lose. This should be a small percentage of your account balance (usually 1-2%). Set your stop-loss order at this level so that the trade automatically exits if the market moves against you. By doing this, you prevent a small loss from turning into a large one.

Place Stops Based on Market Conditions, Not Emotion:
Stop-loss levels should be based on market structure, such as support and resistance levels or volatility, rather than arbitrary figures. For example, place your stop slightly below a support level in a long trade. Avoid setting stops too tight, as normal market fluctuations could trigger them prematurely.

Never Remove or Widen Your Stop-Loss:
Once a stop-loss is set, don't remove it or widen it in hopes that the market will turn in your favor. This is a common mistake traders make when they become emotionally attached to a trade. A stop-loss is your safeguard against significant losses—trust it.

Utilize Trailing Stops:
As the trade moves in your favor, you can use a trailing stop to lock in profits while still giving the trade room to breathe. A trailing stop adjusts your stop-loss price as the market moves, allowing you to maximize gains while still protecting your capital.

3. Focus on Long-Term Profitability: Prioritize Consistency Over Short-Term Gains

Consistent profitability is the true hallmark of successful trading, not winning every trade. The focus should be on the long game, which means accumulating small, consistent profits over time, rather than seeking large, quick wins.

How to Prioritize Long-Term Profitability:

Set Realistic Expectations:
It's crucial to have a realistic outlook on how much you can make in trading. Rather than aiming for massive profits on every trade, focus on making small, consistent gains. Even if your win rate is 50%, if you manage your losses well and let your winners run, you will be profitable in the long run.

Risk-Reward Ratio:
Aim for trades where the potential reward is at least twice the risk (2:1 ratio or higher). This ensures that even if you lose more trades than you win, your winners will cover your losses and still leave you in profit.

Compound Your Returns:
One of the most powerful ways to achieve long-term profitability is through compounding. As you grow your account, reinvest a portion of your profits into future trades. This allows your account balance to grow exponentially over time, even with small percentage gains.

Track Your Performance:
Keep a trading journal where you record not only your wins and losses but also the reasons behind each trade, the market conditions, and your emotional state. Over time, this will give you invaluable insights into your trading habits and performance, helping you refine your strategy for long-term success.

Don't Chase Quick Wins:
The temptation to go for "home run" trades—those that promise big returns in a short amount of time—can lead to taking excessive risks. Instead, stay focused on high-probability setups that align with your strategy. The key is to grow your account slowly and steadily over time.

Final Thoughts
The myth that successful traders win every trade can be detrimental to your growth as a trader. The reality is that even the best traders experience losses, but their success comes from managing those losses effectively and focusing on long-term profitability. By accepting losses, using stop-loss orders to protect your capital, and prioritizing consistent gains over large, risky bets, you can improve your overall performance and achieve success in the markets. Remember, trading is a marathon, not a sprint, and consistent risk management is the key to reaching the finish line profitably.

MYTH #7 – YOU NEED TO PREDICT THE MARKET TO MAKE MONEY

One of the biggest misconceptions is that traders need to predict the market perfectly to make money. That's simply not true. It's impossible to predict market movements with complete accuracy, and trying to do so will only lead to frustration.

Instead, successful traders focus on managing risk and positioning themselves for favorable outcomes. They understand that it's about probability, not certainty. I never try to predict the market; I focus on creating a strategy that adapts to different conditions.

Actionable Steps: How to Trade Successfully Without Predicting the Market

Rather than trying to predict where the market will go, successful traders embrace uncertainty and rely on risk management and adaptability to profit. Below are detailed steps to help you shift from a prediction mindset to a probability-focused, adaptable approach:

1. Embrace Uncertainty: Don't Try to Predict Market Moves—React to Them

It's impossible to know exactly what the market will do next, but you can prepare for various outcomes and react in a way that improves your probability of success. Here's how:

Focus on Probabilities, Not Certainties:
Understand that every trade has a probability of success and failure. You don't need to know where the market will go exactly, but you should understand the likelihood of certain outcomes based on your analysis. This is where the concept of risk/reward comes into play.

Use Technical and Fundamental Analysis as a Guide, Not a Crystal Ball:
While technical indicators and charts can provide valuable insight, they shouldn't be used to "predict" the future. Instead, use them to identify high-probability setups. Look for trends, support/resistance levels, or key events, and position yourself accordingly. Remember, these tools give you probabilities, not certainties.

Accept Market Volatility:
The market is inherently volatile, and trying to predict its every move can be mentally exhausting. Instead of fighting volatility, embrace it by designing a trading plan that works in various market conditions. Whether the market moves up, down, or sideways, your focus should be on managing risk, not predicting the next big swing.

Stay Flexible:
Rather than getting stuck on a specific market direction, be open to changing your perspective as new information comes in. If a trade starts going against you, don't cling to the hope that the market will turn in your favour. Be willing to cut your losses and

move on.

2. Risk Management: Always Have a Clear Plan for What to Do When Trades Go Against You

The difference between a successful and unsuccessful trader often lies in how they manage risk. You will lose trades—what matters is keeping those losses small while allowing your winners to run. Here's how you can protect yourself:

Define Risk Before Every Trade:
Before entering any trade, know exactly how much you're willing to risk. This is usually a small percentage of your total trading capital, often between 1-2%. This ensures that even a string of losses won't wipe out your account.

Use Stop-Loss Orders:
One of the most effective tools in risk management is the stop-loss order. Set this before you even enter a trade. Your stop-loss should be placed at a logical level, such as below support in a long trade or above resistance in a short trade. Never widen your stop-loss in the hope of avoiding a loss.

Position Sizing:
Position sizing is the process of adjusting the size of your trades based on the size of your account and the amount of risk you're willing to take. Use a percentage of your account (such as 1%) to calculate the size of your trades. For example, if you have a $10,000 account and are risking 1%, you would risk $100 on that trade. This keeps your losses manageable.

Plan for Different Scenarios:
Always have a plan for various market scenarios. What will you do if the trade moves in your favor? What if it moves against you? Having predefined plans for different situations will help you remain calm and prevent emotional decision-making. If the market conditions change, be ready to adapt quickly.

3. Adapt and React: Adjust Your Strategy as the Market Evolves
The market is dynamic, and conditions can change rapidly. A rigid strategy may work in some environments but fail in others. To stay profitable, you must learn to adapt and evolve with the market.

Back test and Forward-Test Your Strategy:
Ensure that your strategy works across various market conditions by back testing it against historical data. This will give you confidence that your approach is sound. Additionally, forward-test it in live markets using a demo account or with small amounts of capital to see how it holds up in real-time.

Stay Informed on Market Conditions:
The market is influenced by numerous factors such as news events, economic data, and global trends. Stay updated on current events and market sentiment. If your strategy is based on certain conditions (e.g., a trending market), you may need to adjust or sit out when those conditions change (e.g., during a period of consolidation).

Diversify Your Strategies:
No single strategy works in all market conditions. Some may perform well in trending markets, while others work better in ranging or volatile environments. Develop and maintain a few strategies that you can switch between based on the market conditions. For example, if the market is volatile, you may use a breakout strategy, while in quieter markets, you may rely on range trading.

Be Open to Adjusting Your Strategy:
A strategy that worked well six months ago may not be as effective today. Keep reviewing and refining your strategy over time. If you notice certain elements are consistently underperforming, don't be afraid to tweak them or remove them altogether. Trading is a

continual process of learning and adaptation.

Final Thoughts

The myth that you need to predict the market to make money is a trap that can lead to frustration and poor trading decisions. Instead of trying to guess the market's every move, focus on reacting to what the market gives you. Use probability, risk management, and adaptability as your tools for success. By embracing uncertainty and learning to manage it, you can thrive in an environment where other traders struggle to survive.

The most successful traders don't predict the future—they manage risk, stay flexible, and make decisions based on probabilities. Let the market guide your actions, rather than your predictions.

MYTH #8 – YOU HAVE TO FIND THE PERFECT TRADE ENTRY

Trying to find the perfect entry point is a common mistake for many traders, myself included early on. But there's no such thing as a "perfect" entry. What matters more is how you manage the trade once you're in it.

I've spent years perfecting my ability to manage trades, not just enter them. Entry is just one part of the equation—your ability to handle the position, manage your risk, and know when to exit is what truly makes a difference.

Actionable Steps: Moving Beyond the Quest for the Perfect Trade Entry
Many traders fall into the trap of believing that if they can just find the perfect entry point, success will follow. However, the reality is that trade management is far more critical than entry precision. Here are detailed actionable steps to help you shift your focus from obsessing over entries to effectively managing trades:

1. Don't Obsess Over Entries: Focus on Overall Trade Management
While entry points are important, they should not consume your

entire focus. Here's how to maintain a broader perspective:

Accept Imperfection:
Recognize that no entry is flawless. Even the most experienced traders will occasionally enter a trade too early or too late. Accepting this fact will free you from the stress of finding the "perfect" entry and allow you to concentrate on other vital aspects of trading.

Emphasize Trade Management:
Shift your focus from solely finding an ideal entry point to managing your trade effectively. This includes monitoring your position, adjusting stop-loss orders, and making informed decisions about taking profits or cutting losses. Your ability to adapt during the trade can often mean the difference between a winning and losing trade.

Develop a Trade Routine:
Create a structured routine for managing trades after entry. This routine should include regular checks of your position and market conditions, ensuring you maintain awareness of how the trade is progressing. By standardizing this process, you can remove emotional decision-making and make more rational choices.

2. Plan Your Exits: Have a Clear Exit Strategy Before Entering Any Trade

A well-thought-out exit strategy can often be more valuable than the entry itself. Here's how to plan your exits effectively:

Determine Your Profit Targets:
Before entering a trade, decide at what price level you will take profits. This could be based on resistance levels, Fibonacci retracements, or specific risk/reward ratios. Knowing your exit points in advance will help you avoid greed and panic when the trade moves in your favor.

Set Stop-Loss Orders:
Establish clear stop-loss orders before you enter a trade. This not only protects your capital but also takes the emotional element out of the decision-making process. Determine the level at which you will exit the trade if it goes against you, and stick to this plan.

Use Trailing Stops:
Consider implementing trailing stops to lock in profits as the trade moves favorably. A trailing stop allows you to set a stop-loss order at a percentage or dollar amount below the market price. This way, if the price rises, your stop-loss adjusts upward, protecting your profits while still allowing for potential further gains.

Be Prepared for Changes:
Market conditions can change rapidly. If your initial profit targets or stop-loss levels no longer make sense based on market dynamics, be prepared to adjust them. Flexibility is key, but make sure any adjustments are made based on a rational analysis, not emotions.

3. Monitor Risk/Reward: Ensure the Risk/Reward Ratio is Favourable

Understanding and managing the risk/reward ratio is crucial to successful trading. Here's how to evaluate this effectively:

Calculate Your Risk/Reward Ratio:
Before entering a trade, assess your potential risk against the reward. A common benchmark is to aim for a minimum of a 1:2 ratio (risking $1 to potentially make $2). This ensures that even if you lose more trades than you win, your profitable trades will outweigh the losses.

Evaluate Trade Setups:
Always consider the risk/reward ratio when evaluating trade setups. If the potential reward does not justify the risk you're

taking, it might be wise to pass on that trade. A favourable risk/reward setup can also provide more confidence in executing the trade.

Reassess During the Trade:
As the trade progresses, keep an eye on your risk/reward setup. If the market moves significantly in your favour, reassess your profit target and stop-loss levels. You may want to lock in profits by adjusting your stop-loss to breakeven or trailing the stop as the price moves favourably.

Document and Analyse:
Maintain a trading journal to track your risk/reward ratios and trade outcomes. Analysing your trades will help you identify patterns over time, enabling you to refine your approach. Review your past trades to see where your risk/reward ratios were favorable and how that impacted your results.

Final Thoughts
The belief that a "perfect" entry point is necessary for trading success can lead to frustration and missed opportunities. By shifting your focus to trade management, planning your exits, and monitoring your risk/reward ratios, you'll enhance your overall trading performance.

Trade management is where the real skill lies. Perfect entries may be tempting, but your ability to manage trades effectively will determine your long-term success as a trader. Focus on what happens after you enter a trade, and you will find that success becomes a more attainable goal.

MYTH #9 – THE MORE COMPLICATED YOUR STRATEGY, THE BETTER YOUR RESULTS

Early in my career, I believed that a more complex strategy would lead to better results. I'd create intricate systems with multiple indicators and factors. However, over time, I learned that simplicity often wins in trading.

Complicated strategies can lead to confusion, over-analysis, and mistakes. Some of the most successful traders in the world use simple, easy-to-follow strategies. The key is to master the basics and apply them consistently. In fact, I've seen traders perform worse when they try to juggle too many variables.

Actionable Steps: Embracing Simplicity in Your Trading Strategy

In the world of trading, it's easy to fall into the trap of thinking that a more complex strategy will yield better results. However, simplicity often leads to clarity and better decision-making. Here are detailed actionable steps to simplify your trading strategy for improved performance.

1. Simplify Your Strategy: Focus on Core Concepts
To build a strong trading foundation, concentrate on a few core concepts that are essential to understanding market behaviour:

Identify Key Support and Resistance Levels:
Support and resistance levels are critical for understanding price behaviour. Take time to identify these levels on your charts. Use horizontal lines to mark significant price points where the market has previously reversed or consolidated. This will help you determine potential entry and exit points.

Understand Market Trends:
Familiarize yourself with the concept of trends (uptrends, downtrends, and sideways). Use simple trend lines to visualize the direction of the market. This understanding will guide your trading decisions, helping you identify whether to take long or short positions based on the prevailing trend.

Prioritize Risk Management:
Develop a solid risk management plan that includes setting stop-loss orders and defining your position size. Understanding how much of your capital you are willing to risk on each trade is crucial. For instance, consider risking only 1-2% of your account on any single trade to protect your capital.

Create a Basic Trading Plan:
Outline a straightforward trading plan that includes your entry and exit criteria, risk management rules, and trade evaluation process. This plan should be easy to follow and allow for consistency in your trading approach.

2. Avoid Over-Optimization: Don't Overcomplicate Your Approach

Complicating your trading strategy can lead to analysis paralysis and poor decision-making. Here's how to avoid that:

Limit the Number of Indicators:
Instead of relying on multiple indicators that may contradict each other, select a few that you find useful and stick with them. For example, you might choose one momentum indicator (like the RSI) and one trend-following indicator (like a moving average) to provide clear signals without overwhelming yourself.

Establish Clear Entry and Exit Signals:
Define straightforward rules for entering and exiting trades based on your chosen indicators. This reduces ambiguity and makes it easier to take action. For instance, you might decide to enter a trade when the price crosses above a moving average and exit when it hits a certain profit target or a stop-loss level.

Trust Your Instincts:
Sometimes, the best trades are the simplest ones. Don't overthink your trades by constantly second-guessing yourself. Trust your established rules and the analysis you've conducted. If a trade setup aligns with your strategy, take it without over-analyzing.

3. Test Simpler Systems: Run Backtests on Simpler Strategies
Testing and validating your strategies are crucial steps in ensuring their effectiveness:

Use Historical Data for Back testing:
Back test your simplified strategies using historical price data to see how they would have performed in various market conditions. This can help you identify potential strengths and weaknesses in your approach. Many trading platforms offer built-in back testing tools to facilitate this process.

Evaluate Performance Metrics:
After back testing, analyse key performance metrics such as win

rate, average win/loss, and maximum drawdown. This will help you understand the potential profitability and risk associated with your simpler strategy. Focus on strategies that consistently yield positive results over time.

Iterate and Refine:
Based on your back testing results, make adjustments to your strategy as needed. Keep it simple—if a particular setup consistently underperforms, consider modifying or eliminating it. Remember, the goal is to create a strategy that is both effective and easy to execute.

Implement in Real-Time:
Once you're satisfied with your back testing results, begin to implement your simplified strategy in real-time trading. Start with a demo account or small position sizes to gain confidence without risking significant capital.

Final Thoughts
Simplicity in trading often leads to clarity and better results. By focusing on core concepts, avoiding over-optimization, and testing simpler strategies, you can build a robust trading approach that allows for consistent performance. Embrace the idea that less can be more, and you may find that your trading becomes not only more successful but also less stressful.

MYTH #10 – YOU NEED TO FOLLOW EVERY BIT OF FINANCIAL NEWS & CONSTANTLY WATCH THE MARKETS TO SUCCEED

The idea that you need to be glued to the screen, consuming every bit of financial news, and watching the markets 24/7 is another common misconception. While staying informed is important, overloading yourself with information can lead to analysis paralysis.

The truth is, once you have a solid trading strategy, you don't need to be constantly watching the markets or consuming every news headline. Focus on the news and data that matter to your strategy. I've learned that maintaining a balanced approach prevents burnout and improves long-term performance.

Actionable Steps: Managing Market Information for Trading Success

In the fast-paced world of trading, it can be tempting to immerse yourself in every piece of financial news and market movement. However, this can lead to overwhelming information and poor decision-making. Here's how to manage your market engagement effectively without getting bogged down.

1. Set Time Limits: Dedicate Specific Times for Market Research and Trade Execution

To prevent information overload and enhance productivity, establish clear boundaries around your trading activities:

Create a Daily Schedule:
Allocate specific blocks of time each day for market analysis, trade execution, and reviewing your trading plan. For example, you might set aside 30 minutes in the morning to check overnight market movements and news, followed by another 30 minutes in the evening to review your trades and plan for the next day.

Use a Timer:
Implement a timer during your research sessions to keep yourself accountable. This helps you focus during that time and encourages you to be efficient. If you find yourself going down a rabbit hole of unnecessary information, the timer serves as a reminder to refocus.

Take Breaks:
Incorporate short breaks between your trading sessions to prevent burnout. A brief walk or a change of scenery can refresh your mind and help maintain clarity in your decision-making process.

2. Focus on What Matters: Follow Key Indicators and News Events Relevant to Your Trading Style

Rather than trying to keep up with every headline, concentrate on information that directly impacts your trading strategy:

Identify Relevant News Sources:
Curate a list of trusted financial news sources that provide information relevant to your trading style. This could include economic calendars, newsletters, and analysis from experts. Make a habit of checking these sources at your designated research times.

Track Key Economic Indicators:
Familiarize yourself with the economic indicators that influence your trading decisions. For instance, if you trade Forex, focus on interest rates, employment data, and inflation reports that impact currency values. Set alerts for these key indicators to stay informed without needing constant updates.

Filter Out Noise:
Avoid getting sidetracked by sensational headlines or news that doesn't align with your trading plan. Use a simple rule of thumb: if the news does not directly affect your current positions or trading strategy, consider it background noise and move on.

3. Automate When Possible: Use Alerts and Automation to Help You Stick to Your Strategy
Leverage technology to streamline your trading process and reduce the need for constant market monitoring:

Set Price Alerts:
Utilize price alert features on your trading platform to notify you when an asset reaches a certain price level. This allows you to react promptly to potential trade opportunities without needing to monitor the market constantly.

Automate Trading Strategies:
If your trading strategy allows, consider using automated trading systems or algorithms. These tools can execute trades based on predefined criteria, ensuring you stick to your strategy without

being glued to the screen.

Use Trading Journals:
Keep a digital or physical trading journal to record your trades, insights, and reflections. This helps you maintain a long-term perspective on your performance without needing to constantly analyze market conditions. Regularly review your journal during your scheduled research time to identify patterns and areas for improvement.

Final Thoughts
Success in trading does not require constant vigilance over the markets or an overload of information. By setting time limits, focusing on relevant news, and leveraging automation, you can streamline your trading process, reduce stress, and maintain a balanced approach. This will ultimately lead to improved performance and longevity in your trading journey.

11: THE PATH TO BECOMING A BETTER TRADER

Debunking these myths is just the beginning of your journey to becoming a more effective trader. Trading is a skill that takes time, discipline, and patience to master. Whether you're a beginner or have been in the markets for a while, understanding these truths can help you refine your strategy and approach.

Remember, trading is not about finding shortcuts or quick wins. It's about learning, adapting, and staying consistent over the long term. As you continue to grow as a trader, stay committed to improving your skills, managing your risk, and sticking to your plan. The road to success is long, but with the right mindset, it's achievable.

EPILOGUE

As we conclude our exploration of the myths that often cloud our understanding of trading, I want to take a moment to reflect on the journey we've undertaken together. Trading is not just a profession; it's a mindset—a commitment to growth, learning, and resilience.

Throughout this book, we have dismantled the common misconceptions that can trap even the most passionate traders. From the allure of quick wealth to the misguided belief that trading is merely a gamble, we have examined how these myths can create obstacles on the path to success. Each myth we debunked serves as a reminder that true mastery in trading requires not just knowledge of strategies and techniques, but a profound understanding of ourselves and the markets we engage with.

The insights shared in these pages are a culmination of my experiences—both the victories that fueled my passion and the failures that shaped my perspective. I hope they resonate with you, providing a foundation upon which you can build your own trading journey.

As you move forward, I encourage you to embrace the lessons learned here. Be vigilant against the myths that may resurface, and remain committed to the pursuit of knowledge. Trading is a continuous journey, one that evolves with each new market cycle. The more you learn, the more equipped you will be to navigate the complexities of the financial world.

Remember, success in trading is not defined by how many trades you win but by how well you manage your risk, how disciplined you remain, and how adaptable you are to changing market conditions. Let these principles guide you as you forge your path in the trading arena.

Thank you for joining me on this journey. I am excited to see where your newfound understanding takes you. May you embrace the truth, challenge the myths, and cultivate the mindset that will lead you to lasting success in your trading endeavors.

Here's to your future as a confident, informed, and successful trader!

— GODFX

AFTERWORD

As we reach the end of *10 Myths of Trading Debunked*, I want to take a moment to reflect on the journey we've shared together. The insights and lessons outlined in this book are not merely theoretical; they are grounded in my personal experiences—my triumphs and, yes, my failures.

In the ever-evolving world of trading, the truths we uncover can serve as guiding stars in a landscape often clouded by misconceptions. It is my hope that the myths we've dissected have opened your eyes to the realities of trading and empowered you to approach the markets with renewed clarity and confidence.

Trading is not a destination; it's a continuous journey of growth and self-discovery. The lessons learned from the myths we explored will stay with you as you navigate the complexities of the markets. Remember, every trader faces challenges, but it is your response to those challenges that will ultimately define your success.

As you move forward, I encourage you to embrace the importance of a solid mindset and disciplined approach. Stay curious, remain adaptable, and never stop seeking knowledge. The markets are constantly changing, and those who thrive are those who commit to lifelong learning and personal development.

I want to express my gratitude to you for taking the time to engage with this book. Your commitment to understanding the truths behind the myths is commendable and will serve you well on your trading journey. Remember, you are not alone; there is a vast community of traders who share similar struggles and aspirations. Together, we can learn, grow, and achieve the financial independence we strive for.

Thank you for allowing me to share my experiences and insights with you. May you find success and fulfillment in your trading endeavors, and may the truths you've discovered here guide you toward building a prosperous future.

Here's to your continued growth and success in the world of trading!

— GODFX

AFTERWORD

Lorem ipsum dolor sit amet, consectetur adipiscing elit, sed do eiusmod tempor incididunt ut labore et dolore magna aliqua. Ut enim ad minim veniam, quis nostrud exercitation ullamco laboris.

ACKNOWLEDGEMENT

Writing *10 Myths of Trading Debunked* has been an incredible journey, one that I could not have undertaken alone. I want to express my heartfelt gratitude to everyone who has supported me throughout this process.

First and foremost, I would like to thank my family and friends for their unwavering encouragement and belief in my vision. Your support has been a constant source of strength, reminding me that pursuing this project was worth every moment of dedication and hard work.

To my mentors and fellow traders, thank you for sharing your insights, experiences, and wisdom. Your willingness to challenge my perspectives and offer constructive feedback has profoundly shaped the content of this book. Each discussion, whether in person or online, has added depth and clarity to my understanding of trading, and I am grateful for your guidance.

I would also like to acknowledge the trading community at large. Your stories of triumphs and challenges have inspired me and fueled my desire to create a resource that can help others navigate the complexities of the markets. The shared experiences we have as traders create a powerful network of learning, and I am honored to be a part of it.

Additionally, I want to thank my editor and the publishing team for their expertise and support in bringing this book to life. Your meticulous attention to detail and commitment to quality have been invaluable in ensuring that my message resonates with readers.

Finally, a special thanks to you, the reader. Your curiosity and commitment to understanding the truths behind the myths of trading are commendable. I hope this book serves as a valuable resource on your journey to becoming a more informed and successful trader.

Thank you for joining me on this adventure, and may the insights you gain from this book empower you to achieve your trading goals.

— GODFX

ABOUT THE AUTHOR

Godfx

GODFX is a highly successful trader and financial educator with over a decade of experience in the financial markets. With a background that spans various trading styles—including day trading, swing trading, and long-term investing—GODFX has developed a unique approach to navigating the complexities of the trading world.

Driven by a passion for helping others succeed, GODFX has dedicated much of their career to sharing valuable insights and lessons learned from both triumphs and setbacks. Through a combination of analytical rigor and psychological resilience, they have cultivated a reputation for understanding not just the mechanics of trading but also the mindset required for success.

Having faced the challenges and pitfalls that many traders encounter, GODFX understands the importance of mastering effective habits. Their commitment to continuous learning and personal growth has led to a wealth of knowledge that they are eager to share with aspiring traders.

As a sought-after speaker and mentor, GODFX has inspired countless individuals to adopt disciplined trading practices and cultivate the habits necessary for long-term success in the markets. This ebook is the culmination of years of experience, research, and reflection, aimed at providing readers with practical strategies to enhance their trading effectiveness.

When not trading or educating others, GODFX enjoys engaging with the trading community, exploring new market trends, and continuously refining their own trading strategies. They believe that trading is not just a profession but a lifelong journey of learning and self-discovery.

PRAISE FOR AUTHOR

GODFX is a true visionary in the world of trading. His deep knowledge, passion, and commitment to sharing his expertise have not only transformed his own life but continue to inspire countless others on their trading journeys.
— ANONYMOUS

A masterful guide! GODFX breaks down complex trading concepts into simple, actionable steps. His insights into building a legacy through trading are both profound and practical. This book is a must-read for anyone serious about financial freedom.
— ANONYMOUS

GODFX's approach to trading is as empowering as it is effective. He not only teaches how to succeed in the markets but how to grow as a person. This is more than a book about trading; it's about building a life of purpose.
—ANONYMOUS

Rarely do you find someone as dedicated to helping others achieve their potential in trading as GODFX. His passion for teaching and sharing his knowledge is evident in every chapter. This book will change the way you view trading.
—ANONYMOUS

BOOKS IN THIS SERIES

The Trading Matrix: Breaking The Code To Financial Freedom

Imagine a world where the financial markets are no longer a mystery, but a matrix of opportunities waiting to be unlocked. In The Trading Matrix, GODFX pulls back the curtain on the complex systems that drive market movements, revealing a hidden code that, when understood, can unlock the path to financial freedom. This groundbreaking guide breaks away from traditional trading books, offering a fresh perspective on the art and science of profitable trading. Whether you're a beginner or an experienced trader, this book will challenge everything you think you know about the markets and provide you with the strategies, tools, and mindset needed to decode the market's secrets and achieve consistent success. Are you ready to break free and master The Trading Matrix?

10 Habits Of Highly Effective Traders

Unlock Your Trading Potential with "10 Habits of Highly Effective Traders"!

Are you ready to elevate your trading game? In this essential guide, GODFX, a seasoned trader with over a decade of experience, reveals the ten crucial habits that distinguish successful traders from the rest. Drawing from personal experiences and hard-won lessons, this book provides practical strategies that can transform your trading approach and lead to lasting success.

What You'll Learn:•

Discipline and Consistency: Discover how maintaining a disciplined mindset can enhance your decision-making and help you stick to your trading plan, even in volatile markets.

Risk Management: Learn essential techniques for managing risk effectively, ensuring that you protect your capital while maximizing your potential returns.

Continuous Learning: Embrace the importance of lifelong learning in trading, including how to stay informed about market trends and improve your skills.

Emotional Resilience: Develop the psychological strength needed to navigate the emotional ups and downs of trading, allowing you to make sound decisions under pressure.

Adaptability: Understand the necessity of being flexible and adapting your strategies to the ever-changing market environment.

Whether you are a novice trader looking to build a solid foundation or an experienced trader seeking to refine your approach, "10 Habits of Highly Effective Traders" provides actionable insights that will empower you to reach new heights in your trading journey.

Join thousands of successful traders who have transformed their trading practices with these essential habits. Take the first step toward mastering the art of trading today!

Get your copy now and unlock the habits that lead to trading success!

10 Reasons Why Trading Is The Best Job

10 Reasons Why Trading Is The Best Job is your ultimate guide to understanding why trading is not just a profession, but a life-changing journey. In a world where conventional careers often lead to dissatisfaction and limitations, trading offers a unique opportunity for financial independence, personal growth, and unparalleled freedom.

In this inspiring book, you'll discover:

* Unlimited Income Potential: Learn how trading can empower you to break free from traditional salary constraints and tap into a world of limitless earnings.

* Flexibility and Independence: Explore how trading allows you to design your own schedule, work from anywhere, and truly take control of your life.

* Constant Learning and Growth: Dive into the continuous learning journey that trading offers, helping you develop invaluable skills that extend far beyond the markets.

* Personal Development: Understand how trading challenges you to confront your fears, build discipline, and cultivate resilience.

* Impactful Wealth Creation: Discover how you can create meaningful wealth not only for yourself but also for your community.

This book is packed with practical insights, motivational stories, and actionable advice that will inspire both aspiring traders and seasoned professionals. Whether you're considering trading as a career or looking to deepen your existing knowledge, 10 Reasons Why Trading Is The Best Job will guide you on your path to success and fulfillment.

Unlock your potential and step into a world where the possibilities are endless. Transform your life through trading and discover why it truly is the best job you can have!

Perfect for:

* Aspiring traders
* Financial enthusiasts

* Anyone seeking freedom and personal growth
Take the first step toward your trading journey today!

10 Mistakes Highly Effective Traders Avoid

Are you ready to elevate your trading game and achieve success in the financial markets? 10 Mistakes Highly Effective Traders Avoid is your essential guide to navigating the pitfalls that can hinder your progress and learning from the lessons of a world-class trader.

In this compelling book, GODFX, the No. 1 trader in the world, shares his invaluable insights gained from years of experience in the fast-paced trading arena. With a unique blend of personal anecdotes and practical strategies, this book outlines the top 10 mistakes that even seasoned traders often make—and how you can avoid them.

Inside, you will discover:

* Risk Management: Learn the importance of protecting your capital and how to implement effective risk management strategies.
* Market Psychology: Understand the emotional traps that can cloud your judgment and derail your trading performance.
* Discipline and Planning: Discover the power of a well-structured trading plan and the discipline required to stick to it.
* Adapting to Change: Gain insights on how to stay flexible in an ever-evolving market landscape.

Each chapter offers actionable advice and practical tools that will empower you to develop a disciplined approach to trading. Whether you're a novice just starting or an experienced trader looking to refine your skills, this book will help you build a solid foundation for long-term success.

Why read this book?

* Learn from the triumphs and mistakes of one of the world's top traders.
* Transform setbacks into stepping stones toward your trading goals.

* Cultivate a growth mindset that embraces continuous learning and adaptation.

Don't let common trading mistakes hold you back from achieving your financial dreams. Join GODFX on this transformative journey and unlock the strategies that will set you on the path to becoming a world-class trader.

10 Myths Of Trading Debunked

Unlock the secrets to trading success with 10 Myths of Trading Debunked! In this eye-opening book, renowned trader GODFX takes you on a journey to dismantle the misconceptions that hold traders back from achieving their financial goals.

Are you tired of struggling in the markets? Do you feel overwhelmed by conflicting advice and false narratives? It's time to cut through the noise and discover the truth behind the myths that can derail your trading journey.

In 10 Myths of Trading Debunked, you will learn:

* The Realities Behind Common Misconceptions: Each chapter dives deep into a widely-held myth, exposing the truths that can transform your trading mindset and strategies.

* Practical Strategies for Success: Beyond debunking myths, GODFX provides actionable insights and techniques to help you navigate the markets more effectively.

* Personal Stories and Lessons: Benefit from GODFX's years of experience, filled with both triumphs and challenges, as he shares invaluable lessons learned along the way.

Whether you're a beginner looking to build a solid foundation or an experienced trader seeking to refine your approach, this book is your ultimate guide to mastering the art of trading.

Stop letting myths dictate your trading decisions! Equip yourself with the knowledge you need to succeed in the fast-paced world of trading. With 10 Myths of Trading Debunked, you will gain the clarity, confidence, and skills to pursue your financial dreams.

Join GODFX on this transformative journey and break free from the myths that hold you back!

BOOKS BY THIS AUTHOR

10 Habits Of Highly Effective Traders

Unlock Your Trading Potential with "10 Habits of Highly Effective Traders"!

Are you ready to elevate your trading game? In this essential guide, GODFX, a seasoned trader with over a decade of experience, reveals the ten crucial habits that distinguish successful traders from the rest. Drawing from personal experiences and hard-won lessons, this book provides practical strategies that can transform your trading approach and lead to lasting success.

What You'll Learn:·

Discipline and Consistency: Discover how maintaining a disciplined mindset can enhance your decision-making and help you stick to your trading plan, even in volatile markets.

Risk Management: Learn essential techniques for managing risk effectively, ensuring that you protect your capital while maximizing your potential returns.

Continuous Learning: Embrace the importance of lifelong learning in trading, including how to stay informed about market trends and improve your skills.

Emotional Resilience: Develop the psychological strength needed to navigate the emotional ups and downs of trading, allowing you to make sound decisions under pressure.

Adaptability: Understand the necessity of being flexible and adapting your strategies to the ever-changing market environment.

Whether you are a novice trader looking to build a solid foundation or an experienced trader seeking to refine your approach, "10 Habits of Highly Effective Traders" provides actionable insights that will empower you to reach new heights in your trading journey.

Join thousands of successful traders who have transformed their trading practices with these essential habits. Take the first step toward mastering the art of trading today!

Get your copy now and unlock the habits that lead to trading success!

10 Reasons Why Trading Is The Best Job

10 Reasons Why Trading Is The Best Job is your ultimate guide to understanding why trading is not just a profession, but a life-changing journey. In a world where conventional careers often lead to dissatisfaction and limitations, trading offers a unique opportunity for financial independence, personal growth, and unparalleled freedom.
In this inspiring book, you'll discover:
* Unlimited Income Potential: Learn how trading can empower you to break free from traditional salary constraints and tap into a world of limitless earnings.
* Flexibility and Independence: Explore how trading allows you to design your own schedule, work from anywhere, and truly take control of your life.
* Constant Learning and Growth: Dive into the continuous learning journey that trading offers, helping you develop

invaluable skills that extend far beyond the markets.
* Personal Development: Understand how trading challenges you to confront your fears, build discipline, and cultivate resilience.
* Impactful Wealth Creation: Discover how you can create meaningful wealth not only for yourself but also for your community.

This book is packed with practical insights, motivational stories, and actionable advice that will inspire both aspiring traders and seasoned professionals. Whether you're considering trading as a career or looking to deepen your existing knowledge, 10 Reasons Why Trading Is The Best Job will guide you on your path to success and fulfillment.

Unlock your potential and step into a world where the possibilities are endless. Transform your life through trading and discover why it truly is the best job you can have!

Perfect for:
* Aspiring traders
* Financial enthusiasts
* Anyone seeking freedom and personal growth

Take the first step toward your trading journey today!

10 Mistakes Highly Effective Traders Avoid

Are you ready to elevate your trading game and achieve success in the financial markets? 10 Mistakes Highly Effective Traders Avoid is your essential guide to navigating the pitfalls that can hinder your progress and learning from the lessons of a world-class trader.

In this compelling book, GODFX, the No. 1 trader in the world, shares his invaluable insights gained from years of experience in the fast-paced trading arena. With a unique blend of personal anecdotes and practical strategies, this book outlines the top 10 mistakes that even seasoned traders often make—and how you can avoid them.

Inside, you will discover:
* Risk Management: Learn the importance of protecting your

capital and how to implement effective risk management strategies.
* Market Psychology: Understand the emotional traps that can cloud your judgment and derail your trading performance.
* Discipline and Planning: Discover the power of a well-structured trading plan and the discipline required to stick to it.
* Adapting to Change: Gain insights on how to stay flexible in an ever-evolving market landscape.
Each chapter offers actionable advice and practical tools that will empower you to develop a disciplined approach to trading. Whether you're a novice just starting or an experienced trader looking to refine your skills, this book will help you build a solid foundation for long-term success.
Why read this book?
* Learn from the triumphs and mistakes of one of the world's top traders.
* Transform setbacks into stepping stones toward your trading goals.
* Cultivate a growth mindset that embraces continuous learning and adaptation.
Don't let common trading mistakes hold you back from achieving your financial dreams. Join GODFX on this transformative journey and unlock the strategies that will set you on the path to becoming a world-class trader.

10 Myths Of Trading Debunked

Unlock the secrets to trading success with 10 Myths of Trading Debunked! In this eye-opening book, renowned trader GODFX takes you on a journey to dismantle the misconceptions that hold traders back from achieving their financial goals.

Are you tired of struggling in the markets? Do you feel overwhelmed by conflicting advice and false narratives? It's time to cut through the noise and discover the truth behind the myths that can derail your trading journey.

In 10 Myths of Trading Debunked, you will learn:

The Realities Behind Common Misconceptions: Each chapter dives deep into a widely-held myth, exposing the truths that can transform your trading mindset and strategies.
Practical Strategies for Success: Beyond debunking myths, GODFX provides actionable insights and techniques to help you navigate the markets more effectively.
Personal Stories and Lessons: Benefit from GODFX's years of experience, filled with both triumphs and challenges, as he shares invaluable lessons learned along the way.
Whether you're a beginner looking to build a solid foundation or an experienced trader seeking to refine your approach, this book is your ultimate guide to mastering the art of trading.

Stop letting myths dictate your trading decisions! Equip yourself with the knowledge you need to succeed in the fast-paced world of trading. With 10 Myths of Trading Debunked, you will gain the clarity, confidence, and skills to pursue your financial dreams.

Join GODFX on this transformative journey and break free from the myths that hold you back!

UNTITLED

10 Lessons From Highly Effective Traders
Top 10 Strategies Used by the World's Best Traders
Top 10 Trading Psychology Tips to Master
Top 10 Trading Mindsets
Top 10 Reasons Why 99% of New Traders Lose Money
Top 10 Ways New Traders Can Be Profitable
Top 10 Ways to Create a Winning Trading Plan
Top 10 Ways to Elevate Your Trading Skills
Top 10 Steps to Start Trading & What to Watch Out For
Top 10 Fundamental & Technical Analysis Strategies Used by the World's Best Traders
Top 10 Risk Management Strategies Used by the World's Best Traders
Top 10 Things To Do To Be Number 1 Trader

The markets are more than a collection of numbers; they mirror our decisions, values, and aspirations. In trading, we pursue more than profit—we strive to create opportunities, inspire others, and build a lasting legacy for future generations of traders. Each trade represents a step toward shaping the future we envision.

www.ingramcontent.com/pod-product-compliance
Lightning Source LLC
Chambersburg PA
CBHW070346230526
45471CB00006B/2442